My Song Lyrics Journal

By: Janet Alston Jackson

published by:

SELF AWARENESS TRAININGS, LLC

[ISBN-9780963408693]

photos and images by:
Stock Image
Stuart Miles
Digitalart
Thaikrit
Grant Cochrane

Paperback Edition

Manufactured in the United States of America

DEDICATED TO:

Write Girls a non-profit creative writing and mentoring organization that promotes creativity, critical thinking and leadership skills to empower teen girls.

Visit: WriteGirl.org

(a portion of the proceeds of each book will go to Write Girl)

also visit:

SportingtheRightAttitude.com

TABLE OF CONTENTS

Songs You Love and Your Feelings:
(Fill in the song title to find later)

Songs You Love and Your Feelings:
(fill in the blank lines)

_____55

_____61

_____67

_____73

_____79

_____85

_____91

_____97

_____103

_____109

_____115

_____121

_____127

Make Up Your Own Song Lyrics.................133

List Songs You Write Here:

Your Songs: Page Number
_____   _____

_____   _____

_____   _____

_____   _____

_____   _____

_____   _____

_____   _____

_____   _____

_____   _____

PUBLISHERS NOTES

Disclaimer

This publication is intended to provide helpful and informative material. It is not intended to diagnose, treat, cure, or prevent any health problem or condition, nor is intended to replace the advice of a physician. No action should be taken solely on the contents of this book. Always consult your physician or qualified health-care professional on any matters regarding your health and before adopting any suggestions in this book or drawing inferences from it.

The author and publisher specifically disclaim all responsibility for any liability, loss or risk, personal or otherwise, which is incurred as a consequence, directly or indirectly, from the use or application of any contents of this book.

MUSIC QUOTES

"People haven't always been there for me but music always has." ~Taylor Swift

"Music is the art of thinking with sounds."
~Jules Combarieu

"Music is what feelings sound like."
~Bo Bennett

Words make you think a thought. Music makes you feel a feeling. A song makes you feel a thought."
~E.Y. Harburg

"One good thing about music, when it hits you, you feel no pain." ~Bob Marley

"Music is love in search of a voice." ~Leo Tolstoy

"Where words fail, music speaks." ~Hans Christian Anderson

"All music comes from God."~ Johnny Cash

"Everything in the universe has a rhythm, everything dances."~Maya Angelou

"A great song should lift your heart, warm the soul and make you feel good."~Colbie Caillat

WHERE TO FIND FREE LYRICS TO YOUR FAVORITE SONGS ONLINE:

http://www.lyrcsdome.com

http://www.elyrics.net

http://www.metrolyrics.com

http://www.lyricsmode.com

My Favorite Music Artists

_

HOW DOES MUSIC MAKE YOU FEEL?

_____

_____

_____

_____

_____

_____

_____

_____

_____

_____

_____

_____

_____

SONG:_____

ARTIST:_____

LYRICS:

_____

_____

_____

_____

_____

_____

_____

_____

_____

_____

_____

What thoughts or memories does the song make you think about? You can also make up your own lyrics to the song here:

Date:_____

_____

_____

_____

_____

_____

_____

_____

_____

_____

_____

_____

_____

_____

_____

_____

Circle What Your Feeling(s) Looks Like

Name and Circle Your Feeling(s)
(You Can Have More Than One Feeling At A Time)

love	hurt	fear	hate
worry	shame	gloom	angry
guilty	caring	warm	sad
brave	shy	patient	jealous
sympathy	confused	happy	moody
excited	frustrated	sensitive	embarrass
understand	encouraged	discouraged	playful

DRAW YOUR FEELINGS OR PLACE A PHOTO HERE

SONG:_____

ARTIST:_____

LYRICS:

_____

_____

_____

_____

_____

_____

_____

_____

_____

What thoughts or memories does the song make you think about? You can also make up your own lyrics to the song here:

Date:_____

_____

_____

_____

_____

_____

_____

_____

_____

_____

_____

_____

_____

_____

_____

_____

_____

Circle What Your Feeling(s) Looks Like

Name and Circle Your Feeling(s)
(You Can Have More Than One Feeling At A Time)

love	hurt	fear	hate
worry	shame	gloom	angry
guilty	caring	warm	sad
brave	shy	patient	jealous
sympathy	confused	happy	moody
excited	frustrated	sensitive	embarrass
understand	encouraged	discouraged	playful

DRAW YOUR FEELINGS OR PLACE A PHOTO HERE

SONG:_____

ARTIST:_____

LYRICS:

_____

_____

_____

_____

_____

_____

_____

_____

_____

_____

_____

_____

_____

What thoughts or memories does the song make you think about? You can also make up your own lyrics to the song here:

Date:_____

_____

_____

_____

_____

_____

_____

_____

_____

_____

_____

_____

_____

_____

_____

_____

_____

_____

Circle What Your Feeling(s) Looks Like

Name and Circle Your Feeling(s)
(You Can Have More Than One Feeling At A Time)

love	hurt	fear	hate
worry	shame	gloom	angry
guilty	caring	warm	sad
brave	shy	patient	jealous
sympathy	confused	happy	moody
excited	frustrated	sensitive	embarrass
understand	encouraged	discouraged	playful

DRAW YOUR FEELINGS OR PLACE A PHOTO HERE

SONG:_____

ARTIST: _____

LYRICS:

_____

_____

_____

_____

_____

_____

_____

_____

_____

_____

_____

What thoughts or memories does the song make you think
about? You can also make up your own lyrics to the song here:

Date:_____

_____

_____

_____

_____

_____

_____

_____

_____

_____

_____

_____

_____

_____

_____

_____

_____

Circle What Your Feeling(s) Looks Like

Name and Circle Your Feeling(s)
(You Can Have More Than One Feeling At A Time)

love	hurt	fear	hate
worry	shame	gloom	angry
guilty	caring	warm	sad
brave	shy	patient	jealous
sympathy	confused	happy	moody
excited	frustrated	sensitive	embarrass
understand	encouraged	discouraged	playful

DRAW YOUR FEELINGS OR PLACE A PHOTO HERE

SONG:_____

ARTIST:_____

LYRICS:

_____

_____

_____

_____

_____

_____

_____

_____

_____

_____

_____

_____

_____

What thoughts or memories does the song make you think about? You can also make up your own lyrics to the song here:

Date:_____

_____

_____

_____

_____

_____

_____

_____

_____

_____

_____

_____

_____

_____

_____

_____

Circle What Your Feeling(s) Looks Like

Name and Circle Your Feeling(s)
(You Can Have More Than One Feeling At A Time)

love	hurt	fear	hate
worry	shame	gloom	angry
guilty	caring	warm	sad
brave	shy	patient	jealous
sympathy	confused	happy	moody
excited	frustrated	sensitive	embarrass
understand	encouraged	discouraged	playful

DRAW YOUR FEELINGS OR PLACE A PHOTO HERE

SONG:_____

ARTIST:_____

LYRICS:

_____

_____

_____

_____

_____

_____

_____

_____

_____

_____

_____

_____

What thoughts or memories does the song make you think about? You can also make up your own lyrics to the song here:
Date:_____

_____

_____

_____

_____

_____

_____

_____

_____

_____

_____

_____

_____

_____

_____

_____

_____

Circle What Your Feeling(s) Looks Like

Name and Circle Your Feeling(s)
(You Can Have More Than One Feeling At A Time)

love	hurt	fear	hate
worry	shame	gloom	angry
guilty	caring	warm	sad
brave	shy	patient	jealous
sympathy	confused	happy	moody
excited	frustrated	sensitive	embarrass
understand	encouraged	discouraged	playful

DRAW YOUR FEELINGS OR PLACE A PHOTO HERE

SONG:_____

ARTIST:_____

LYRICS:

_____

_____

_____

_____

_____

_____

_____

_____

_____

_____

_____

_____

What thoughts or memories does the song make you think
about? You can also make up your own lyrics to the song here:
Date:_____

_____

_____

_____

_____

_____

_____

_____

_____

_____

_____

_____

_____

_____

_____

_____

_____

Circle What Your Feeling(s) Looks Like

Name and Circle Your Feeling(s)
(You Can Have More Than One Feeling At A Time)

love	hurt	fear	hate
worry	shame	gloom	angry
guilty	caring	warm	sad
brave	shy	patient	jealous
sympathy	confused	happy	moody
excited	frustrated	sensitive	embarrass
understand	encouraged	discouraged	playful

DRAW YOUR FEELINGS OR PLACE A PHOTO HERE

SONG:_____

ARTIST:_____

LYRICS:

_____

_____

_____

_____

_____

_____

_____

_____

_____

_____

_____

_____

What thoughts or memories does the song make you think about? You can also make up your own lyrics to the song here:

Date:_____

_____

_____

_____

_____

_____

_____

_____

_____

_____

_____

_____

_____

_____

_____

_____

Circle What Your Feeling(s) Looks Like

Name and Circle Your Feeling(s)
(You Can Have More Than One Feeling At A Time)

love	hurt	fear	hate
worry	shame	gloom	angry
guilty	caring	warm	sad
brave	shy	patient	jealous
sympathy	confused	happy	moody
excited	frustrated	sensitive	embarrass
understand	encouraged	discouraged	playful

DRAW YOUR FEELINGS OR PLACE A PHOTO HERE

SONG:_____

ARTIST:_____

LYRICS:

_____

_____

_____

_____

_____

_____

_____

_____

_____

_____

_____

_____

What thoughts or memories does the song make you think about? You can also make up your own lyrics to the song here:

Date:_____

_____

_____

_____

_____

_____

_____

_____

_____

_____

_____

_____

_____

_____

_____

_____

_____

Circle What Your Feeling(s) Looks Like

Name and Circle Your Feeling(s)
(You Can Have More Than One Feeling At A Time)

love	hurt	fear	hate
worry	shame	gloom	angry
guilty	caring	warm	sad
brave	shy	patient	jealous
sympathy	confused	happy	moody
excited	frustrated	sensitive	embarrass
understand	encouraged	discouraged	playful

DRAW YOUR FEELINGS OR PLACE A PHOTO HERE

SONG:_____

ARTIST:_____

LYRICS:

_____

_____

_____

_____

_____

_____

_____

_____

_____

_____

_____

_____

What thoughts or memories does the song make you think about? You can also make up your own lyrics to the song here:

Date:_____

_____

_____

_____

_____

_____

_____

_____

_____

_____

_____

_____

_____

_____

_____

_____

_____

Circle What Your Feeling(s) Looks Like

Name and Circle Your Feeling(s)
(You Can Have More Than One Feeling At A Time)

love	hurt	fear	hate
worry	shame	gloom	angry
guilty	caring	warm	sad
brave	shy	patient	jealous
sympathy	confused	happy	moody
excited	frustrated	sensitive	embarrass
understand	encouraged	discouraged	playful

DRAW YOUR FEELINGS OR PLACE A PHOTO HERE

SONG:_____

ARTIST:_____

LYRICS:

_____

_____

_____

_____

_____

_____

_____

_____

_____

_____

_____

_____

What thoughts or memories does the song make you think about? You can also make up your own lyrics to the song here:

Date:_____

_____

_____

_____

_____

_____

_____

_____

_____

_____

_____

_____

_____

_____

_____

_____

_____

Circle What Your Feeling(s) Looks Like

Name and Circle Your Feeling(s)
(You Can Have More Than One Feeling At A Time)

love	hurt	fear	hate
worry	shame	gloom	angry
guilty	caring	warm	sad
brave	shy	patient	jealous
sympathy	confused	happy	moody
excited	frustrated	sensitive	embarrass
understand	encouraged	discouraged	playful

DRAW YOUR FEELINGS OR PLACE A PHOTO HERE

SONG:_____

ARTIST:_____

LYRICS:

_____

_____

_____

_____

_____

_____

_____

_____

_____

_____

_____

_____

_____

What thoughts or memories does the song make you think about? You can also make up your own lyrics to the song here:

Date:_____

_____

_____

_____

_____

_____

_____

_____

_____

_____

_____

_____

_____

_____

_____

_____

_____

Circle What Your Feeling(s) Looks Like

Name and Circle Your Feeling(s)
(You Can Have More Than One Feeling At A Time)

love	hurt	fear	hate
worry	shame	gloom	angry
guilty	caring	warm	sad
brave	shy	patient	jealous
sympathy	confused	happy	moody
excited	frustrated	sensitive	embarrass
understand	encouraged	discouraged	playful

DRAW YOUR FEELINGS OR PLACE A PHOTO HERE

SONG:_____

ARTIST:_____

LYRICS:

_____

_____

_____

_____

_____

_____

_____

_____

_____

_____

_____

What thoughts or memories does the song make you think about? You can also make up your own lyrics to the song here:

Date:_____

_____

_____

_____

_____

_____

_____

_____

_____

_____

_____

_____

_____

_____

_____

_____

_____

Circle What Your Feeling(s) Looks Like

Name and Circle Your Feeling(s)
(You Can Have More Than One Feeling At A Time)

love	hurt	fear	hate
worry	shame	gloom	angry
guilty	caring	warm	sad
brave	shy	patient	jealous
sympathy	confused	happy	moody
excited	frustrated	sensitive	embarrass
understand	encouraged	discouraged	playful

DRAW YOUR FEELINGS OR PLACE A PHOTO HERE

SONG:_____

ARTIST:_____

LYRICS:

_____

_____

_____

_____

_____

_____

_____

_____

_____

_____

_____

_____

What thoughts or memories does the song make you think about? You can also make up your own lyrics to the song here:

Date:_____

_____

_____

_____

_____

_____

_____

_____

_____

_____

_____

_____

_____

_____

_____

_____

_____

Circle What Your Feeling(s) Looks Like

Name and Circle Your Feeling(s)
(You Can Have More Than One Feeling At A Time)

love	hurt	fear	hate
worry	shame	gloom	angry
guilty	caring	warm	sad
brave	shy	patient	jealous
sympathy	confused	happy	moody
excited	frustrated	sensitive	embarrass
understand	encouraged	discouraged	playful

DRAW YOUR FEELINGS OR PLACE A PHOTO HERE

SONG:_____

ARTIST:_____

LYRICS:

_____

_____

_____

_____

_____

_____

_____

_____

_____

_____

_____

What thoughts or memories does the song make you think about? You can also make up your own lyrics to the song here:

Date:_____

_____

_____

_____

_____

_____

_____

_____

_____

_____

_____

_____

_____

_____

_____

_____

_____

Circle What Your Feeling(s) Looks Like

Name and Circle Your Feeling(s)
(You Can Have More Than One Feeling At A Time)

love	hurt	fear	hate
worry	shame	gloom	angry
guilty	caring	warm	sad
brave	shy	patient	jealous
sympathy	confused	happy	moody
excited	frustrated	sensitive	embarrass
understand	encouraged	discouraged	playful

DRAW YOUR FEELINGS OR PLACE A PHOTO HERE

SONG:_____

ARTIST:_____

LYRICS:

_____

_____

_____

_____

_____

_____

_____

_____

_____

_____

_____

_____

_____

What thoughts or memories does the song make you think about? You can also make up your own lyrics to the song here:

Date:_____

_____

_____

_____

_____

_____

_____

_____

_____

_____

_____

_____

_____

_____

_____

_____

_____

Circle What Your Feeling(s) Looks Like

Name and Circle Your Feeling(s)
(You Can Have More Than One Feeling At A Time)

love	hurt	fear	hate
worry	shame	gloom	angry
guilty	caring	warm	sad
brave	shy	patient	jealous
sympathy	confused	happy	moody
excited	frustrated	sensitive	embarrass
understand	encouraged	discouraged	playful

DRAW YOUR FEELINGS OR PLACE A PHOTO HERE

SONG:_____

ARTIST:_____

LYRICS:

_____

_____

_____

_____

_____

_____

_____

_____

_____

_____

_____

_____

_____

What thoughts or memories does the song make you think about? You can also make up your own lyrics to the song here:

Date:_____

_____

_____

_____

_____

_____

_____

_____

_____

_____

_____

_____

_____

_____

_____

_____

_____

Circle What Your Feeling(s) Looks Like

Name and Circle Your Feeling(s)
(You Can Have More Than One Feeling At A Time)

love	hurt	fear	hate
worry	shame	gloom	angry
guilty	caring	warm	sad
brave	shy	patient	jealous
sympathy	confused	happy	moody
excited	frustrated	sensitive	embarrass
understand	encouraged	discouraged	playful

DRAW YOUR FEELINGS OR PLACE A PHOTO HERE

SONG:

ARTIST:

LYRICS:

What thoughts or memories does the song make you think about? You can also make up your own lyrics to the song here:

Date:_____

_____

_____

_____

_____

_____

_____

_____

_____

_____

_____

_____

_____

_____

_____

_____

_____

_____

Circle What Your Feeling(s) Looks Like

Name and Circle Your Feeling(s)
(You Can Have More Than One Feeling At A Time)

love	hurt	fear	hate
worry	shame	gloom	angry
guilty	caring	warm	sad
brave	shy	patient	jealous
sympathy	confused	happy	moody
excited	frustrated	sensitive	embarrass
understand	encouraged	discouraged	playful

DRAW YOUR FEELINGS OR PLACE A PHOTO HERE

SONG:_____

ARTIST:_____

LYRICS:

_____

_____

_____

_____

_____

_____

_____

_____

_____

_____

_____

_____

_____

What thoughts or memories does the song make you think about? You can also make up your own lyrics to the song here:

Date:_____

_____

_____

_____

_____

_____

_____

_____

_____

_____

_____

_____

_____

_____

_____

_____

_____

Circle What Your Feeling(s) Looks Like

Name and Circle Your Feeling(s)
(You Can Have More Than One Feeling At A Time)

love	hurt	fear	hate
worry	shame	gloom	angry
guilty	caring	warm	sad
brave	shy	patient	jealous
sympathy	confused	happy	moody
excited	frustrated	sensitive	embarrass
understand	encouraged	discouraged	playful

DRAW YOUR FEELINGS OR PLACE A PHOTO HERE

SONG:_____

ARTIST:_____

LYRICS:

_____

_____

_____

_____

_____

_____

_____

_____

_____

_____

_____

_____

What thoughts or memories does the song make you think about? You can also make up your own lyrics to the song here:

Date:_____

_____

_____

_____

_____

_____

_____

_____

_____

_____

_____

_____

_____

_____

_____

_____

_____

Circle What Your Feeling(s) Looks Like

Name and Circle Your Feeling(s)
(You Can Have More Than One Feeling At A Time)

love	hurt	fear	hate
worry	shame	gloom	angry
guilty	caring	warm	sad
brave	shy	patient	jealous
sympathy	confused	happy	moody
excited	frustrated	sensitive	embarrass
understand	encouraged	discouraged	playful

DRAW YOUR FEELINGS OR PLACE A PHOTO HERE

This Section Is For You To Write

Your Song Lyrics

Made in the USA
Columbia, SC
11 October 2017